A COMPANY OF
OWNERS

Maximizing Employee Engagement

DAREN MARTIN, PhD

A Company of Owners

Published by Clovercroft Publishing, Franklin, Tennessee

Cover and Interior Design by Tamyra McCartney-Burleson

Illustration of Dr. Martin (p. 6) by Madison Martin

Illustrations by John Pechacek

Additional Design by Will von Bolton

Edited by Tammy Kling

Printed in the United States of America

978-1-942557-34-0

CONTENTS

8 — Fire Your Employees

26 — Company Culture

40 — Mantra VS Mission

46 — How Are Team
Members Viewed?

84 — Hire the Right People

102 — Keep the Right People

112 — Manager Mentality
Leading Owners

136 — Command and Control
or Collaboration

148 — Being an Owner

"I WILL HAVE NO MAN WORK FOR ME WHO HAS NOT THE CAPACITY TO BECOME A PARTNER."

—J.C. PENNEY

WHO AM I?

I'm a leadership and management consultant who has logged over a million miles traveling to hundreds of corporations across the globe, to deliver this message to thousands of employees.

PARTNERSHIPS WORK BETTER THAN DICTATORSHIPS.

This is a wake-up call to leaders. Let's work together to create a company of owners where employees are engaged in your results.

— Daren Martin

FIRE YOUR EMPLOYEES.

NO, SERIOUSLY.

Employees are a thing of the past. Employees are a drain on your company. High-performing companies hire and develop owners.

THE
QUESTION

While speaking to more than 70 senior level executives of very large companies, I asked:

"How many of you would say you work in a predominantly 'owner culture' company?"

How many do you think raised their hand?
A WHOPPING ZERO!

MEET
STACEY

SHE IS ENGAGED.

- She puts in a reasonable amount of hours but accomplishes a lot.

- When she runs up against a barrier, she removes it.

- She motivates herself and does not need someone to tell her what to do and when to do it.

- She takes charge of important goals and doesn't wait for permission.

- She has fun at work.

- She comes up with new ideas.

- She improves inefficient processes.

- She produces.

STACEY CONTRIBUTES TO YOUR SUCCESS AS A COMPANY

AND MAKES YOU MONEY.

WORK

MEET
CRAWLEY

HE IS A ZOMBIE EMPLOYEE.

- He moves; he shuffles.
- When he runs up against a barrier (like a chain link fence in a zombie movie), he stops, paralyzed with what to do. He doesn't go around it, look for fence cutters, or crawl over it. He just pushes up against it, hoping that more zombies will join and the sheer weight will bring it down.
- He lives to eat, and in zombie-employee world, eating is his paycheck.
- His mind disengaged a long time ago.
- He lives for the weekend.
- He goes through the motions hoping no one notices.
- He generates zero new ideas and zero improvements to the process.

CRAWLEY MAKES YOUR COMPANY WORSE
AND LOSES YOU MONEY.

ACT :

MAKE A LIST OF YOUR TOP FIVE
CRAWLEYS AND STACEYS
AT YOUR COMPANY.

A GALLUP POLL SHOWED THAT IN
THE AVERAGE COMPANY, ROUGHLY
29% OF EMPLOYEES
ARE TRULY ENGAGED.

That means a lot of zombies are walking your halls.

LESS THAN 1/3 OF YOUR WORKFORCE IS ENGAGED?

THAT'S LIKE. . .

A six-cylinder engine with only two cylinders working

A tricycle with one wheel

A one-legged stool

A guitar with only two strings

Most companies are operating significantly below their capacity due to a disengaged workforce.

If only a third of the workforce is engaged, either you have hired all the wrong people (not likely) or the company culture is not reinforcing engagement and producing an Owner mentality.

Either way, it leaves you incredibly handicapped to try to do all of the work with only a third of your engine operating at full capacity.

Years ago, "Made in Japan" was synonymous with "Piece Of Crap." "Made in Japan" now represents high quality products like Lexus, Honda, Sony, etc. And it wasn't because Japanese companies swapped out their Japanese workers for foreigners who produced better products. What changed was the work philosophy, processes, systems, & company culture at some of their key companies! Same workers, very different outcomes.

WHY VALUE OWNERS?

When you have a company of owners. . .

- Many eyes are focused on the business, not just the manager's eyes.

- Leaders are developed at every level, resulting in incredible bench strength.

- You get true continuous improvement.

- Accountability is high and driven at lower levels.

- Waste is reduced.

- More is accomplished and produced.

EMPLOYEES FEEL ENTITLED.
OWNERS FEEL EMPOWERED.

There is a BIG difference. Entitled people are always looking out for what you are going to give them. They look for handouts. They talk a lot about what you "owe" them.

Owners feel empowered. They get by giving. They are naturally rewarded by their performance and the value they provide the company. They perform because it is who they are, and they reap rewards accordingly.

Owners take care of the business as if it belongs to them.

OWNERS UNDERSTAND THE CONCEPT OF

PERFORMANCE BEFORE PROMOTION

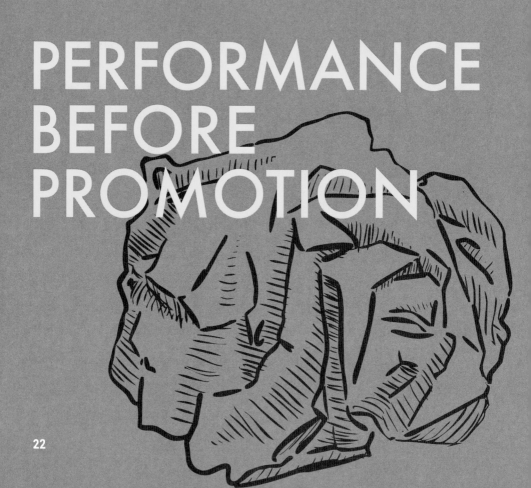

EXPERIMENT

Researchers threw a piece of paper in the hallway of a busy office. When someone stopped to pick it up (most did not), the researchers interviewed them and asked why they had picked up the trash and had thrown it away. Most of the respondents said something like, "This is my place and I want to keep it nice."

In short, the ones who stopped and picked up the wad of paper had an OWNER mentality.

If they stop to pick paper up in the hallway, what else are they doing to watch out for and take care of the company?

ACT:

TRY DOING THIS EXPERIMENT AT WORK, AND SEE WHAT KIND OF RESPONSE YOU GET.

COMPANY
CULTURE

Author and thought leader Blake Leath was once asked:

"WHAT CAN WE DO TO GET OUR EMPLOYEES MORE ENGAGED?"

His response:

"I WOULDN'T BOTHER."

He went on to point out that if your company's system, culture, and ethos don't engage people already, then trying to "pump the employees up" in some kind of a "rah, rah" fashion is not going to work. You have to create a company culture that taps into people's desire to succeed.

COMPANY CULTURE BEGINS WITH

VISION

A CLEAR VISION IS PARAMOUNT.

Owner companies have a clear direction that is understood by everyone throughout the company. They have a shared vision, which is meaningful and attainable. A clear company vision should drive behavior at every level.

A STUDY WITH OVER 23,000 WORKERS, MANAGERS AND EXECUTIVES REVEALED THAT...

- Only 17 percent felt their organization fosters open communication that is respectful of differing opinions and that results in new and better ideas.

- Only 10 percent felt that their organization holds people accountable for results.

- Only 13 percent have high-trust, highly cooperative working relationships with other groups or departments.[1]

Just because leaders know what the vision is doesn't mean everyone else does.

[1] From the Harris Interactive and FranklinCovey "xQ (Execution Quotient) Questionnaire," 2004, in Steven R. Covey, The 8th Habit, (New York: Free Press, 2004), 2-3.

"If you want to build a ship, don't drum up people together to collect wood, and don't assign them tasks and work, rather, teach them to long for the endless immensity of the sea."

—ANTOINE DE SAINT-EXUPERY

Dynamic leaders tell stories; they paint imaginable pictures of the future, and they inspire people to act.

Mediocre leaders assign a bunch of tasks and get caught up in the daily activities of the business.

Great leaders are great storytellers!

"SCRATCH THE SURFACE IN A TYPICAL BOARDROOM AND WE'RE ALL JUST CAVEMEN* WITH BRIEFCASES, HUNGRY FOR A WISE PERSON TO TELL US STORIES"

—ALAN KAY

* and cavewomen (addition mine)

"MAKE NO LITTLE PLANS, THEY HAVE NO MAGIC TO STIR MEN'S BLOOD."

—DANIEL BURNHAM

STOP. PAUSE.
THINK.

How does what you have read so far inspire you to think differently about your business?

MANTRA VS. MISSION

Guy Kawasaki points out companies need a mantra, not a mission.

A mission statement is a bunch of management words on the wall that don't tend to drive action.

Example:

"Our mission is to provide a superior customer service experience by utilizing our years of experience to enrich our community and employees through providing a quality . . . "

POKE ME IN THE EYE WITH A STICK!

A mantra directs actual behavior. It tells you how to act, what to do, what to make a priority, and so much more.

THE RITZ-CARLTON®
mantra is

"WE ARE LADIES AND GENTLEMEN
SERVING LADIES AND GENTLEMEN."

BRILLIANT.

I had a client who had as part of their mission:

"TO BE THE PREMIER REFINING COMPANY. . ."

I suggested this as a litmus test for all behavior and decisions.
This should shape the questions they ask, including

"Is this the way the premier refining company would do it?"

"What would the premier refining company do in this situation?"

"Which of these two candidates would the premier refining company hire?"

A GOOD MANTRA
IS MARCHING ORDERS!

ACT:

HOW ARE TEAM MEMBERS VIEWED?

DOES YOUR COMPANY HAVE DRONES,
CRONES, OR OWNERS?

"WHY, WHEN I ASK FOR A PAIR OF HANDS, DO I GET A BRAIN?"

—HENRY FORD

Toyota gets an average of 40 ideas a year from every employee!

Companies like Toyota developed an "all hands on deck" philosophy which drove a culture of true continuous improvement and a much superior product which has **DOMINATED** the market for **MANY** years.

> *In fairness to Henry Ford, he was trying to create an assembly line in an age of craftsmen. He needed consistency and didn't want workers thinking. He wanted his workers to only do what they were told. After manufacturing matured, the idea of a mindless workforce became a liability.*

OWNERSHIP CULTURES VALUE AND REWARD
PERFORMERS, OUTLIERS, AND VISIONARIES

I made the following statement to two different company leaders:

"YOU WANT ALL HIGH PERFORMERS."

Leader 1: *"You'll never get all high performers."*

Leader 2: *"Of course we want all high performers."*
(leader 2 is one of the best CEOs in the country)

P.S. Fire Leader 1!

YOU HAVE A TEAM, NOT A FAMILY!

FAMILY

- Born into it
- Have to put up with crazy Uncle Ned
- Not being paid
- Diversity of values tolerated
- Leaders determined by default & family position
- Diversified purpose and direction
- Performance is largely irrelevant

TEAM

- Join or be invited
- Don't have to tolerate crazy (or rude, lazy, etc. . .)
- Being paid to produce results
- Diversity of values disruptive
- Leaders emerge or are elected based on value
- Unified purpose and direction
- Performance is required for continued involvement

FAMILY

When crazy Uncle Ned gets hammered at the family Christmas party and gets all handsy, you shrug your shoulders and say, *"That's crazy Uncle Ned for ya."* **AND**, he is invited back next year.

If Susie keeps sponging off the rest of the family because she *"can't find a job,"* you throw a few bucks her way and hope she leaves you alone.

TEAMS DON'T WORK THAT WAY

A power forward who signs with a basketball team to produce ten rebounds a game will be cut from the team if he only averages two.
IT'S THAT SIMPLE.

People team in order to achieve better results.
A team is only as good as its weakest link.
HIGH-PERFORMING TEAMS HAVE NO WEAK LINKS.

ACT:

ASK YOURSELF,
"AT OUR COMPANY DO WE ACT MORE LIKE A (DYSFUNCTIONAL) FAMILY OR A HIGH-PERFORMING TEAM?"

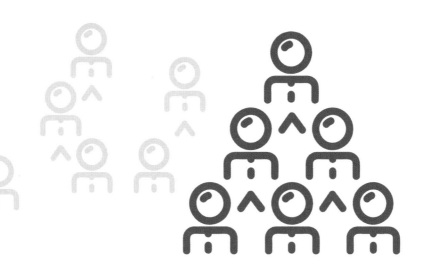

KNOW THE TRUTH

STATED CULTURE

The stated culture is what you see written
on the walls at any given company.
It represents who we say we are.

THE SHHHHH. . .
HIDDEN CULTURE

The hidden culture is the actual
behaviors at any given company.
It reveals who we *really* are.

**High-performing companies have no hidden culture.
What they say is what they do.**

If you do not have a clear and accurate awareness of what is going on at every level of your company, you will be making bad decisions based on bad information.

"THE BEGINNING OF WISDOM IS CALLING THINGS BY THE RIGHT NAME."

—CHINESE PROVERB

I have worked at companies where this appeared to be the attitude:

"THERE IS ONE PERSON AT EVERY COMPANY WHO KNOWS EXACTLY WHAT IS GOING ON. THEY SHOULD BE FIRED IMMEDIATELY."

—UNKNOWN

STOP SHOOTING THE MESSENGER.

Many people at a company know what's broken. Many even know what they would do to fix it. Are you listening? Several years ago, I met with a law partner at his plush downtown firm:

Law Partner: "What are you going to do for our firm?"

Me: "I am going to tell you important things about your company you don't know."

Law Partner: "How are you going to do that?"

Me: "I am going to talk to people who know what is really going on, starting with the receptionist who checked me in."

When you listen with an open mind, people tell you very important information about what is going on at all levels of the company. When I am invited to help shape the culture of a company, the first thing I do is interview a broad cross section of people. I am amazed by how open and willing they are to tell me what is really going on with the company. They talk about what they like but also about their biggest points of frustration and what they think needs to change.

I am equally amazed by the defensiveness I experience when I share my findings with senior executives (anonymously and with a broad stroke so as to protect my sources). I am baffled to hear things like, "That's not what's really going on" or "That's not true" as I share information about "the way things are" from a wide range of credible resources.

If, like an ostrich, you choose to stick your head in the sand to avoid danger, don't expect to provide much leadership to the organization with which you are out of touch.

Can you think of examples in your own company where this might be the case?

"IT IS DIFFICULT TO GET A MAN TO UNDERSTAND SOMETHING WHEN HIS SALARY DEPENDS ON HIS NOT UNDERSTANDING IT."

—UPTON SINCLAIR

I consulted for a company where they published monthly metrics to indicate where each supervisor's department was producing as measured against others. In my conversations with the supervisors, they indicated the numbers were being "fixed" to hit the metrics and said things like, "Give me the number you want me to hit, and I'll hit it." By the way, this was shared with me more as a cry for help than as a secret to be kept. The supervisors were suffering because things were not working well.

MY CONVERSATION WITH THE SENIOR MANAGER:

Me: "This initiative is not working at the level it could be."

Senior Manager: "Yes, it is. There is a 90 percent compliance rate."

Me: "That number is not accurate; they are telling me they are cooking the books."

Senior Manager: "That is impossible to do in this system."

Me: (Insert a look of bewilderment) "Well, possible or not, they are telling me they are playing with the numbers!"

They subsequently stopped publishing the metrics to reduce the pressure to "perform" and focused on the actual performance. Consequently, the reality emerged, and they were able to begin to address the real issues.

SNIPING OF(F) HIGH PERFORMERS

A frontline worker came up with a great idea that saved his company a lot of money. He was given the highest award by the company, publicly thanked by the president in front of his peers, and given a substantial cash reward. It was the last idea he ever brought forward.

WHY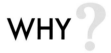

Yep. His coworkers gave him such grief, calling him a "suck up" and "brown noser," that it didn't seem worth it.

FORMULA FOR DISASTER

A BUCKET OF CRABS CULTURE.

The crabs grab other crabs trying to get out of the bucket and pull them down.

A DIFFERENT FORMULA FOR DISASTER

It is even worse when

"BROWN NOSING"

low performers get promoted.

Promote an employee managers love, but fellow employees have no respect for because they schmooze more than they produce, and you will lose respect among the workforce.

Recognize this guy?

My name is 'Dwight'

ELIMINATE SILOS

ELIMINATE US/THEM

When I ask any group of people at a company, "Who here wants the company to fail?" Generally, everyone agrees, "nobody." Once this is established, I drive home the point that "We are on the same team with a common goal."

Most people, from the senior executives down to the newest member of the team, want the company to succeed—even if just for the obvious reason that it is the only way they can keep their job.

Unfortunately, many companies are highly entrenched silos. Individual contributors and team leaders forget the inherent interdependence on other parts of the company. The result is minimal collaboration from one department to the next around very important goals. I have identified multiple Us/Them patterns at a number of different companies.

COMMON US/THEM PATTERNS INCLUDE

- Salary versus Hourly

- Union versus Non Union

- Managers versus Non Managers

- Operations versus Maintenance

- Sales versus Warehouse

- Shareholders versus Employees

- Finance versus Business Development

- Seasoned Employees versus Millennials

A CLEAR EXAMPLE OF AN US/THEM MENTALITY

I had a person write me after a lengthy conversation
to say he had decided to

"give the company a chance."

I wrote him back and said,

"No way! You are not going to give the company a chance.
You ARE the company!"

ACT:

WHAT ARE SOME OBVIOUS US/THEM RELATIONSHIPS AT YOUR COMPANY?

SILO REINFORCERS

We reinforce silos by doing things like incentivizing the sales department to move as much product as they can as quickly as possible, while incentivizing the warehouse to stock as little inventory as possible.

Or incentivizing maintenance to close incomplete work requests versus doing the repair right, resulting in half done jobs for operations.

SILO BUSTERS (Some Ideas)

- Have each department interact with and be able to explain the function of other departments and the value they bring to the company. Possibly have a "day in the field" where they experience other jobs firsthand.

- Encourage cross-department engagement, including lunches and mixed department meetings. Discuss things such as:
  - Our biggest struggle as a department is. . .
  - What we most need from other groups at our company is. . .
  - One way we provide value to the company is. . .
  - We could be a lot more effective as a department if. . .

- Organize cross-functional process teams to address a problem or opportunity of their choosing to "make us better, more profitable, or more efficient as a company."

- Use the term "our" instead of "the" when describing other departments. "Our sales team" versus "the sales team."

- Eliminate the word "they" when referring to decisions made, roadblocks, and other areas. "They won't let us" or "They keep resisting" should be replaced with specific identifying titles and labels. Ask the question, "Whom do you mean by 'they?'"

"UNTIL EVERY TEAM MEMBER VIEWS THE COMPANY AS AN INTERDEPENDENT ENTERPRISE, YOU WILL NEVER HAVE AN OWNER COMPANY."

–Daren Martin

(Yes, I quoted myself in my own book!)

PUSH PLAY.

"The opposite of play isn't work. It's depression. To play is to act out and be willful, exultant and committed as if one is assured of one's prospects."

—BRIAN SUTTON-SMITH

SOUTHWEST AIRLINES PHILOSOPHY

"People rarely succeed at anything unless they are having fun doing it."

"Play will be to the 21st century what work was to the last 300 years of industrial society—our dominant way of knowing, doing and creating value."

—PAT KANE

OLD SCHOOL SAYING "All work and no play makes
Jack a very dull boy."

COMPANY VERSION "All work and no play makes your
company a VERY dull company."

DULL COMPANIES DON'T DOMINATE INDUSTRIES

If people are not having fun at work, chances are you do not have an owner company. High-performing companies are generally fun and enjoyable places to work, no matter how serious the business.

Henry Ford had a no smiling or laughing policy at work. He said "those behaviors" are for after work. In Ford's opinion, work is serious business. Henry Ford did a lot of things right, but when it came to this philosophy, he was dead wrong. People perform better when they're enjoying work.

Create a culture where you have fun at work on purpose. Think about that. . . on purpose fun. Rather than fun being a distraction from your company's purpose, it can be part of the fuel that creates energy around accomplishing your purpose.

POSITIVE PEOPLE PERFORM BETTER

The best workplaces are full of life and energy.

In a productive work group, fun, entertaining, educational, inspirational, and self-development activities can increase employee engagement and remind employees of their value to the organization. Celebration should be a vital part of the work world.

There may be occasion where it makes sense to do something over the weekend or after hours, but for the most part, team building activities should be done during work hours. People spend enough time at work and away from their families. It is a nice break to be able to do something during normal business hours that does not detract from their "outside of work" life.

21 STARTER IDEAS

FOR HOW INDIVIDUALS, MANAGERS, OR TEAMS CAN
CONTRIBUTE TO A GREAT WORK ENVIRONMENT

1. Start a gratitude card that you write to a person. Then have them write to another person and pass it on until the card is filled with thank you messages.

2. Go to a dollar store and buy goofy prizes for coworkers. Use them in a departmental awards show where you pass out awards for various made up categories.

3. Bring donuts, bagels, fresh fruit, etc. on a regular basis.

4. Organize a monthly outing (Burger Wednesdays) to try different burger/pizza/taco/salad places and select a winner at the end of the year. Show up as a team and give the restaurant an award.

5. Organize TED Tuesdays—a brown-bag lunch where you watch a Ted Talk (see Ted.com) and discuss the content of the talk and its value to the individuals and company.

6. Organize an in-office scavenger hunt with a cool prize at the end.

7. Set out a jigsaw puzzle in a common area.

8. Buy some fun stickers and attach them to any Post-It Notes you write.

9. Put on an art show where employees post their original artwork in the break room.

10. Sponsor a talent show and invite other departments.

11. Auction off lunch with the CEO or a local celebrity and give the money to charity.

12. Have employees bring childhood pictures. Post them and have people guess who they are.

13. Create a humor board where jokes and cartoons are posted.

14. Supply flowers for a conference room to brighten up the place.

15. Plan a local field trip to somewhere educational or fun (a museum, gallery, aquarium, federal building, or company providing tours).

16. Organize a book swap where people bring in favorite books and exchange them for coworkers' favorites.

17. Teach hobby or outside interest classes at a lunch and learn (art, sports, or any outside interest in which a coworker has expertise).

18. Have a department pet (a goldfish, hermit crab, puppy, cat, whatever is allowed).

19. Set up a friendly competition with another department.

20. Establish office intramural "sports" where you compete as teams.

21. Appoint a fun chairman or a fun team and have them plan events.

ACT:

MAKE A LIST OF TEN WAYS TO CREATE MORE PLAY AT YOUR COMPANY.

HIRE
RIGHT

THE
PEOPLE

"GET THE RIGHT PEOPLE ON THE BUS."

—JIM COLLINS

It has been said the secret to a successful business is LOCATION, LOCATION, LOCATION!

The real secret to a successful business is
PEOPLE, PEOPLE, PEOPLE.

YOU HAVE TO START WITH THE **RIGHT PEOPLE**.

ASK YOURSELF...

"Of the people on my team, would I hire them again?"

If the answer is no, you have some serious work to do. Manage them up or manage them out.

HIRE DIFFERENCE MAKERS

- Hire people who want to perform, and who strive for success.
- Hire people you trust to get the job done.
- Hire people who can and will own an area of responsibility.

THEN

- Set them up for success.
- Pay these people well.

Make sure you know who the "right people" are and that your
"PICKER ISN'T BROKEN."

I have seen managers who had skewed visions of what they wanted in a workplace, and it completely influenced their hiring and promoting, to the detriment of the organization.

For example, the guy who only promoted "pit bulls" because he wanted managers who could go out and harass the workforce to get results. Clearly, his picker was broken!

THE OSMONDS WERE WRONG!

ONE BAD

*Written by George Jackson

CAN SPOIL THE WHOLE BUNCH

GET RID OF THE WRONG PEOPLE

AND BY THE WRONG PEOPLE I MEAN

— chronic low performers
— poison
— and fish out of water

ACT:

STOP AND THINK—WHO AT YOUR COMPANY CAME TO MIND AS YOU READ THAT LAST PAGE? WHAT ARE YOU GOING TO DO ABOUT IT?

HIRING/MANAGEMENT MISTAKES

- Not cutting your losses early, when it becomes apparent the hire is not a high performer.
- Only hiring people that are just like you.
- Hiring people that won't outperform you or make you look bad.
- Ignoring ambitious or creative people who want to make a difference because they seem too eager or make you uncomfortable.
- Ignoring super smart/humble people who just want to produce, because you don't think they are "dynamic" enough.
- Letting moderate or low performers participate in the interviewing of potential candidates and have a vote in who gets hired.
- Dismissing the "current generation" as low performers rather than matching opportunities and job activities to their strengths.
- Hiring experienced but unambitious people over less experienced visionaries.

TALENT MANAGEMENT

"YOU'RE FINE, YOU'RE FINE, YOU'RE FIRED"

PHENOMENON

Most companies drift along with low performers. They make excuses for them. They give them moderate performance reviews. They tell them they are satisfied with their performance. And then, the day comes when they can no longer tolerate their low performance, and they start down the path of exiting them out of the company.

STOP EVALUATING PERFORMANCE WITH YOUR BRAIN AND START USING YOUR MOUTH.

I had a conversation with a manager who said she was "going to let a person go." I asked, "Do you think she will be shocked, or do you think she will understand given the ongoing feedback you have been giving her?" The manager proclaimed, "We have talked about this so many times; she will understand it is the culmination of my dissatisfaction!" I was not surprised to get the call from the flabbergasted manager a few days later saying the employee burst into tears and declared she "had no idea the dissatisfaction was so serious that her job was in jeopardy."

How did such a big disconnect occur? The manager gave feedback and had the conversation multiple times . . . in her own head. What was conveyed with her words was a much toned down version, leaving the employee clueless to the real severity. I have witnessed this disconnect multiple times.

CONDUCT LEGITIMATE PERFORMANCE REVIEWS.

NO, NOT ONCE A YEAR—DAILY!

Answer this question:

> "Knowing everything I know about this person,
> if they applied today for their current position,
> would I hire them?"

If the answer is no, ask yourself. . .

> "Do they have the fundamental ability to change
> some things that would enable me to say yes?"

If the answer is still no. . .

> Why are you keeping them?

MANAGE UP
OR MANAGE OUT

Evaluate managers not only on their performance but also on the performance of their people. Mandate, insist on, and demand that managers ONLY have strong performers on their team. And, by that, I don't mean PAPER performers (they get high marks on the annual paper review but are mediocre when compared to true high performers).

In sports, coaches are evaluated based on their team's ability to perform. If the team they select and train does well, they do well. If the team does not do well, coaches are held accountable.

OUR TEAM ROCKS!

I was asked to speak with the manager of what was considered by upper management their lowest performing team. When I asked the manager about his team (a maintenance crew), he said his team was "the best."

When we discussed his team members one by one, he confided he was not able to send at least three of the seven team members to do a one-person job. Two of the mechanics had to work with a partner because, if they were not being watched, they would goof off. The third mechanic had to work with a partner because his skills could not be trusted.

AND YET, THIS MANAGER'S ASSESSMENT WAS HE HAD A HIGH PERFORMING TEAM!

WHEN IS THE BEST TIME TO FIRE SOMEONE?

A THE FIRST TIME YOU THINK ABOUT IT!

Chances are, there are people in your company you have NEVER thought about firing. They are rock stars, top performers who demonstrate exceptional skill and are a pleasure to work with.

Others, however, are a constant source of irritation, in constant need of coaching, and barely produce. They present a lot of problems and no solutions. Or they are just generally difficult people to work with who are constantly disrupting the workplace and leaving a trail of bodies in their wake. Don't hang on to low performers or poison.

Netflix has a corporate philosophy that says,

"WE DON'T HIRE BRILLIANT JERKS."

They say the price to their teams is too great,
and I totally agree.

KEEP THE RIGHT PEOPLE

CFO: WHAT IF WE DEVELOP OUR PEOPLE AND THEY LEAVE?

CEO: WHAT IF WE DON'T AND THEY STAY?

"LEADERS ARE MADE, NOT BORN."

—COLIN POWELL

ACT:

ASK YOURSELF

"WHAT ARE WE DOING TO ACTIVELY CREATE LEADERS AT OUR COMPANY? WHAT COULD WE BE DOING?"

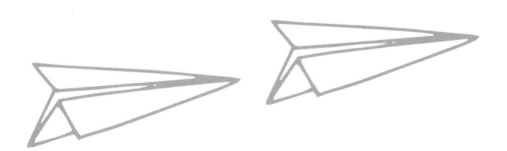

TABLE STAKES

You Get No Credit for

- Reasonable pay
- A non-abusive work environment
- Standard benefits

Those are known as disincentives. People expect them.
If they are not present, their absence creates malcontents.

You lose points for

- Paying below market
- A stressful work environment

You get major points for

- Paying (great performers) a premium
- Creating a work environment where people can succeed often
- Creating a work environment where people want to succeed often
- Providing an enriching, learning and growing environment

These are incentives. People produce at a higher level when
these conditions are present.

"IF YOU
THINK HIRING
PROFESSIONALS
IS EXPENSIVE TRY
HIRING AMATEURS."

—ANONYMOUS

PAY UP

YOU GET WHAT YOU PAY FOR.

Pay your performers! Unapologetically, thankfully, and in a celebrated way! I have seen companies lose high performers over a few dollars. That is truly being a penny wise and a pound foolish.

CASH TIGHT?

Look for other ways to incentivize.
More vacation, work from home, stock options, more autonomy, more input, or whatever is of interest to the person. At a bare minimum, verbally acknowledge that you know they are worth more and that they will eventually be rewarded for "sticking with you."

MANAGER MENTALITY LEADING OWNERS

"I'm slowly becoming a convert to the principle that you can't motivate people to do things, you can only demotivate them. The primary job of the manager is not to empower but to remove obstacles."

—SCOTT ADAMS

"SO MUCH OF WHAT WE CALL MANAGEMENT CONSISTS IN MAKING IT DIFFICULT FOR PEOPLE TO WORK."

—PETER DRUCKER

LEADERS (pick your favorite)

Don't tell people how to do things, tell them what to do, and let them surprise you with their results. –GEORGE PATTON

Leadership is lifting a person's vision to high sights, the raising of a person's performance to a higher standard, the building of a personality beyond its normal limitations. –PETER DRUCKER

Become the kind of leader that people would follow voluntarily; even if you had no title or position. –BRIAN TRACY

People buy into the leader before they buy into the vision. –JOHN MAXWELL

Leadership is the key to 99 percent of all successful efforts. –ERSKINE BOWLES

The first responsibility of a leader is to define reality. The last is to say thank you. In between, the leader is a servant. –MAX DEPREE

A leader is best when people barely know he exists, when his work is done, his aim fulfilled, they will say: we did it ourselves. –LAO TZU

A Leader is a dealer in hope. –NAPOLEON BONAPARTE

My own definition of leadership is this: The capacity and the will to rally men and women to a common purpose and the character, which inspires confidence. –GENERAL MONTGOMERY

BARRIER REMOVAL

MANAGER'S VIEW

In an excellent article called "How Leaders Kill Meaning at Work," Teresa Amabile and Steven Kramer describe a survey done with over 669 managers from a cross section of companies and industries. Managers were asked to rank the importance of these five motivators: incentives, recognition, clear goals, interpersonal support, and progress in the work. The results? Only eight percent of the senior executives ranked progress as the most significant motivator.

REALITY

Contrast that with the results of a multiyear research project Amabile and Kramer describe in their book, The Progress Principle, which revealed that making progress in meaningful work is the most important factor in engaging people in their jobs.[2]

[2] See http://www.mckinsey.com/insights/leading_in_the_21st_century/how_leaders_kill_meaning_at_work

THE BOTTOM LINE ?

Workers are most satisfied when they are able to make progress in their work on a regular basis. Rather than a day filled with bureaucratic and managerial barriers that impede progress, they are able to advance important objectives and see the results.

I am not talking about conceptual or outside barriers which can spur on engagement. These are problems to be solved and barriers to be broken.

I am talking about the stupid stuff like . . .

- "It's not in the budget" (even though there is a guaranteed 10 times ROI).

- "We don't have the manpower" (outsource it if the returns are that significant).

- "That will never get approval."

CURLING

**Have you ever seen the sport of curling?
It's in the Winter Olympics!**

One person slides the stone toward a faraway target. The sweepers, equipped with special sweeping tools (brooms), run ahead of the stone and sweep debris from in front of it to both guide the stone and facilitate its speed. On occasion, they sweep debris in front of the stone to slow it down as it approaches the bullseye.

Q IS A MANAGER THE SWEEPER OR THE STONE THROWER?

I think you can make the argument for both; however, I envision the manager mainly as the sweeper. A manager's job is to remove debris from the efforts of his team and to occasionally slow things down when it is prudent for the desired outcomes.

NOW THAT'S A GREAT QUESTION

To create an owner culture, managers should regularly ask

- What do you need to be even more effective in your job?

- What is getting in the way of you being successful?

- What would you do if you were in charge?

- What would you change?

ACT:

ASK THOSE QUESTIONS TO TEN OF YOUR TEAM MEMBERS.

LISTEN ATTENTIVELY TO THEIR RESPONSES.

WHICH IS A BETTER MOTIVATOR?

NEITHER!

Read Daniel Pink's book *Drive* if you want to understand what really motivates people.

"NOBODY GOES TO WORK TO DO A BAD JOB."

—EDWARD DEMING

No, seriously, it's true.

PEOPLE WANT TO SUCCEED.

They want to put effort in and produce something meaningful.
The best days are the days they walk out the door to head
home and are able to say,

"I DID SOMETHING MEANINGFUL TODAY."

ARE YOU A THEORY X OR THEORY Y COMPANY?

In the book *The Human Side of Enterprise*, written by Douglas McGregor in the '60s, contends that what a manager thinks about workers directly impacts the results they receive. McGregor says managers (and companies) believe one of two very different things about the average worker.

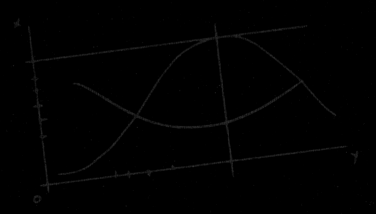

THEORY X

- Work is unenjoyable and something people do because they have to.
- Very few people are creative.
- You have to control people in the workplace.
- The average employee is ambitionless and simply wants to do their job and go home.
- Most employees only care about job security.

THEORY Y

- Work is as enjoyable as play.
- Creative people are in abundance.
- When people are motivated, they will be self-directed.
- Employees who are committed to a set of objectives will seek out responsibility.
- Tangible and intangible rewards including a feeling of achievement, accomplishment, and growth engenders commitment.
- The average person has an incredible capacity for innovation and creativity that is largely untapped.

129

Obviously, what you believe about the average worker will greatly influence the way you lead your people.

Theory X will lead to a more command and control approach, in which you try to keep your people in line.

Theory Y will result in a more collaborative approach, where you consider your employees to be team members and make sincere efforts to include and inspire them.

I asked a disgruntled manager recently why he had not received the help from his team members. He said,

"Because people are lazy and don't want to do their jobs."

Clearly, a Theory X guy.

I went on to coach him that his worldview was greatly limiting his attempts to get support from others and that it was hindering his success. His core belief about people kept him from tapping into the tremendous amount of talent and desire for success in the people around him.

GREAT COMPANY CULTURES PRAISE DILIGENCE OVER SMARTNESS.

"SMART" PEOPLE GIVE UP MORE
QUICKLY THAN TENACIOUS PEOPLE.

Enron was a company full of "smart people."

[
To understand the difference read the book
*Bounce: Mozart, Federer, Picasso,
Beckham, and the Science of Success*
by Matthew Syed.
]

"IT IS A FINE THING TO HAVE ABILITY, BUT THE ABILITY TO DISCOVER ABILITY IN OTHERS IS THE TRUE TEST."

—LOU HOLTZ

PEOPLE ACT THE WAY YOU EXPECT THEM TO ACT.

TRY TREATING THEM
LIKE OWNERS.

"If human beings are perceived as potentials rather than problems, as possessing strengths instead of weaknesses, as unlimited rather than dull and unresponsive, then they thrive and grow to their capabilities."

– BOB CONKLIN

COMMAND AND CONTROL OR COLLABORATION

Throughout history, there have always been (largely insecure) leaders who believed "might was right." They governed through fear and intimidation because they did not have the influence or skills to lead. They demanded a single point of decision-making and direction. All roads led to them since they were the beginning and end of all activity.

AUTHORITARIAN LEADERSHIP

- Their position is their power

- They command people

- They instill fear

- Might over right

- Because I said so

- People do things because they have to

INFLUENCERS

- Their influence is their power

- They lead people

- They inspire

- Right is always right

- Because it is the best thing to do

- People do things because they want to

For more on this, see my book
The Tale of Three Coaches.

YOU THINK THIS IS A NEW IDEA?

In *The Art of War*, the story is told of the general who lowers himself to suck the poison out of a lowly foot soldier's leg. When they write to the foot soldier's mother to describe what honor has been bestowed on her son and her family, she is furious and depressed. When asked "Why?" she responds, "Because years ago the same general did a similar act for my husband and he never stopped following him all the way to his grave."

William Wallace successfully led an army of peasants against the powerful king of England and his formidable army and set things in motion, resulting in the eventual freedom of Scotland from England's tyrannical rule. In the movie portrayal *Braveheart*, King Edward (a.k.a. Longshanks) leads from the rear of the army, sending his own troops into danger, remarking, "We have reinforcements." Meanwhile, William Wallace leads his army into battle from the front. Longshanks has authority; William Wallace has influence.

COMMAND AND CONTROL IS DEAD. PUT A FORK IN IT ALREADY.

In the Civil War, commanders had a very high death rate because they led their armies into battle.[3]

Companies that succeed foster collaboration cultures. They pick the right people, train them well, and then move decision making closer to the valve. But don't take my word for it. Listen to a 37-year Army general:

"Command and control will not serve the future."[4]

—LT. GEN. RUSSEL HONORÉ (RET.)

[3] See Alan Weiss, The Consulting Bible (Hoboken, NJ: John Wiley & Sons, 2011), n.p.

[4] For more, see http://www.businesswithoutborders.com/industries/others-industries/leaders-stuck-on-stupid/

HIRE THE RIGHT PEOPLE. EMPOWER THEM TO DO THEIR JOBS.

Collaborative cultures maximize their performance by empowering people throughout the company to make decisions and lead their part of the operation.

GREAT COMPANY CULTURES ARE COLLABORATIVE.

They develop understanding
through inclusion in
the process.

"TELL ME AND
I WILL FORGET.

SHOW ME AND
I MAY REMEMBER.

INVOLVE ME AND I
WILL UNDERSTAND."

—CHINESE PROVERB

Donald Trump told his first apprentice,

"YOU CAN MAKE A GOOD DECISION OR YOU CAN MAKE A BAD DECISION, BUT THE DAY YOU FAIL TO MAKE A DECISION, YOU ARE FIRED!"

True Empowerment.

Give people the authority, opportunity, and encouragement to make decisions in all areas.

Owner companies don't want "yes" people who are afraid to make a decision. They empower people to decide at their level of involvement without fear of retribution or being second-guessed. Hire the right people, train them well, then let them make decisions!

IN CONTRAST

While working on a culture change initiative at a company, I interviewed a person who had been put in charge of a very large project with a huge budget. He indicated he was being second-guessed at every turn and not being afforded the resources he asked for to make the project a success.

I asked his supervisor a series of questions:

Me: "Do we think Ted is the right guy for the job?"

Supervisor: "Yes."

Me: "Do we think he has the ability to lead a successful project?"

Supervisor: "Yes."

Me: "Then GIVE him what he is asking for!"

BOTTOM LINE

OWNER CULTURES DON'T HAPPEN, THEY ARE CREATED.

EGO IS THE ENEMY OF OWNER CULTURES.

PEOPLE ARE SMART WHEN YOU EXPECT THEM TO BE.

OWNER CULTURES DOMINATE.

BEING AN OWNER

AND LEADING OTHERS TO DO THE SAME

We have talked about the company and its managers. Let's focus a bit on what individuals can do to be an owner and lead others to do the same.

"THE BEST WAY
TO PREDICT
THE FUTURE IS
TO CREATE IT."

—ALAN KAY

ACT:

IN WHAT WAYS ARE YOU CREATING YOUR FUTURE? *IF YOU ARE NOT, WHY NOT START OUTLINING IT NOW?*

"OWNERS" ARE FUNDAMENTALLY DIFFERENT FROM EMPLOYEES.

They have a psychological stake in the success of the company that drives their daily behavior. They treat the company as if it were their own.

Owners. . .

- Take losses personally
- Celebrate successes as if they were their own
- Have an enterprise mentality versus a silo mentality

OWNERS ARE PRICELE$$ AND ESTABLISH THEMSELVES AS

INDISPENSABLE CONTRIBUTORS.

OWNERS GET THINGS DONE

BRING A PLAN, NOT AN IDEA.

Scenario 1

Son: "We need to buy a new lawn mower!"

Dad: "No."

Scenario 2

Son: "I have been monitoring the performance of our lawn mower for two months and its performance is on the decline. Given its current condition and capabilities, it is taking three hours to do our lawn. I researched and found a new mower that is $900. It will mow our lawn in 1.2 hours. I have lined up three other lawns to mow at $40 each, which will generate enough revenue to pay off the mower in less than two months. If you will front me the investment, I will pay the $900 back—plus a 20 percent return in four months."

So I ask you: How would you respond?

GIVE OTHERS SOMETHING TO SAY YES TO.

IT'S EASIER TO SAY YES TO A PLAN THAN AN IDEA.

TRUTH

Initiatives that you have researched and developed that start ten yards from the end zone are more likely to be embraced and adopted than those that are rough ideas with 90 yards to go!

OPPOSITE MEANINGS

I recently posed a situation to a group of managers and employees.

The Scenario:

You share an idea with your manager. The manager shows some interest and encourages you to pursue it. Subsequent email correspondence about the idea is met with no response. How would you interpret this, and what would you do?

Employees Said: "I assume the manager must not be that interested in proceeding, so I would drop it and move on to something else."

Managers Said: "I'm probably really busy and focused on other things. If you think it is important or I showed initial interest, please keep pushing it until you get a response."

The employees' response was in direct contrast to how the managers wanted them to respond.

HOW MANY GREAT IDEAS ARE DROPPED DUE TO THIS PHENOMENON?

THE OWNER MENTALITY

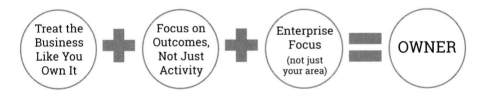

Owners deal with expenses
as if the money were coming
out of their bank account.

Owners get the best deal possible
while also looking to do the right
thing for the company.

This means owners avoid being. . .

"A penny wise and
a pound foolish."

They are more than willing to spend
significant amounts of money when
the ROI makes it worthwhile. Owners
don't refuse to spend when it is in the
companies' best interest just because
they are being cheap or fearful.

161

FIX
BROKEN.

Owners fix broken processes, systems, equipment, etc. rather than just limping along and "making do." Inefficiency kills businesses. Owners seek to eradicate roadblocks and bottlenecks that get in the way of success. They recognize the value in doing things the right way every time.

OWNERS ARE PICKY ABOUT THEIR TEAM.

Owners don't coddle low performers or promote people based purely on seniority. They pick a team they believe will over perform. They hand pick the cream of the crop and empower them to perform.

BUILD YOUR TEAM.
THEN,
BUILD YOUR TEAM.

Once owners have the right people, they continue to tweak, improve, and overhaul the team to produce greater results. Owners make sure they are providing training, resources, time, and whatever else is necessary to develop and empower their team members.

A THOROUGHBRED
CHAMPION WILL
FADE AND FAINT
IF YOU DON'T
FEED HER.

OWNERS SPUR ON TEAM MEMBERS WITH ENCOURAGEMENT WHEN THEY FALTER.

They also praise lavishly and specifically when victories are achieved as well as during the journey.

ACT:

IN WHAT WAYS ARE YOU NURTURING AND DEVELOPING YOUR TEAM?

WHAT ELSE COULD YOU DO?

EXCELLENCE IS NON-NEGOTIABLE

Owners insist on excellence whether it pertains to product quality, people quality, or process quality.

They want the best, work for the best, and accept only the best. Owners also recognize failed attempts as potential steps forward rather than setbacks.

Owners thoughtfully ask these questions when things don't go well. . .

1. Do we know what went wrong?

2. Do we know how to adjust to prevent it in the future?

3. Have we learned something useful?

4. How do we press on?

OWNERS ARE WASTE HATERS

Owners hate to see waste and eliminate it at every opportunity.

CAUTION

Certain expenditures may seem financially extravagant or unnecessary to a "bean counter" but have the potential to provide tenfold returns in performance and production. That is not waste!

DON'T BE GUILTY OF JUMPING OVER DOLLARS TO PICK UP DIMES

OR SAYING, "THE SAVINGS IS ONLY $___? THAT'S NOT THAT BIG A DEAL."

OUTCOME FANATICS

Owners don't just care if tasks are completed. They want to make sure the intended outcomes are achieved. To an owner, the job is not done until the intended outcomes and rewards are fully achieved.

BIG PICTURE THINKERS

Owners think about the enterprise, not just their area. They consider the repercussions of their actions on other parts of the company and the process. They look for enterprise success, not just individual or team accolades. The running back who just set the NFL record but whose team lost the game should be downtrodden, not exuberant.

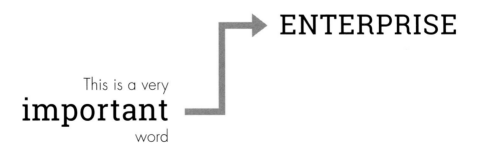

ENTERPRISE

This is a very **important** word

OWNERS ARE INNATELY CURIOUS.

They are not satisfied with the stock or pat answer.
They dig deeper, looking for non-rote responses.

Phrases you will never hear uttered by an owner. . .

- That's the way we have always done it.

- That will never work.

- Why in the world would you want to do it that way?

- Just do it the way you were told.

OWNERS TALK AND ACT LIKE OWNERS

OWNERS ARE NOT COMPLAINERS

Owners address difficulties head on and work to solve them.
They don't whine about how bad things are; they produce solutions.

Work to eliminate the response

"No complaints"

when people ask how you are doing.

[
There has to be a better, more positive metrics
by which to describe your current situation.
]

OWNERS HAVE AN INSATIABLE POSITIVE NATURE AND BELIEVE EVERY PROBLEM CAN BE SOLVED.

"Argue for your limitations and sure enough, they're yours."

—RICHARD BACH

"Obstacles are those frightful things you see when you take your eyes off your goals."

—HENRY FORD

OWNERS DON'T TAKE THEIR EYE OFF THE BALL.

Owners are not distracted by non-essentials or detours.

They recalibrate themselves and others to true north when things start to veer off course. Owners are constantly reprioritizing to ensure energy is being put into the highest return. They have a developed sense for avoiding non-material distractions.

ACT:

WOULD YOU DESCRIBE YOURSELF AS HAVING "AN INSATIABLE POSITIVE NATURE?"

How does your response help or hurt you?

THE CORE

AT THE CORE OF EVERY OWNER ARE EIGHT FUNDAMENTAL CHARACTERISTICS.

Check out these eight core elements and see how you measure up.

ANALYZER

The only thing worse than no data is bad data. Owners don't just churn out bits of data; Owners turn data into meaningful information by considering the embedded truth, pitfalls, and opportunities. They look for first, second, and third order implications of the decisions they make and the actions they take.

INITIATOR

Owners don't ask or wait for the ball; owners grab
the ball and advance it down the field. If owners need
something, they ask. Owners share their ideas while taking
responsibility for them. Along with the idea, they also deliver
well formulated strategies for making it reality. Losers wait
for things to happen; winners make things happen.

STRATEGIC THINKER

Owners refuse to be drones. Owners are never simply order fillers. Owners use their gifts to further the company and its initiatives by thinking creatively about the business, including how to pursue opportunities and address problems encountered.

FORWARD THINKER

Owners learn from the past but are always facing forward. The world and business are in flux. Owners act as a scout, always looking around the corner to see what is coming next, so they can be ahead of the curve. They thrive on "seeing the future" and refuse to rest on past or current laurels.

CONNECTOR

Owners understand their colleagues, supervisor, and those under their care are vital resources and relationships. Owners are most effective when connected with others. Owners are not locked in by departmental boundaries but look for and recognize the value of resources outside their area and even outside the company.

LEARNER

Owners understand that they can only be better if others are looking in on their work and have the freedom and invitation to help them improve. Owners set goals and expect to be measured against the goals they set. This gives them a push when they may not have it otherwise. They are consummate readers and learners.

(readers are leaders)

ACCOUNTABLE

Owners take responsibility for everything in their world all the time. You never hear woulda, shoulda, coulda from owners. They own what they touch. They never point to other people or extenuating circumstances as excuses for not accomplishing what they committed to do.

EMPOWERED

Owners are never stuck. When owners feel stuck, they push through by taking a moment to reflect and invite input from others. They don't wait for someone else to empower them; they empower themselves.

NET-NET

Successful companies seek out, empower, reward, and reinforce the innate desire in every person to be a success. They produce a company of owner/entrepreneurs who are fully engaged and committed to the success of the company, the individuals around them, and themselves. Owner companies thrive and are the present and future of business.

If you want to survive and thrive in the coming years, demonstrate an owner mentality at every turn. Work to establish immense value to your company or organization by thinking and acting like an owner.

re-read this book repeatedly.

— Ed Katz, COO All Star Products Group

A business Bible that will move you to immediately begin to execute its many well-thought ideas and directives!

— Mike Muhney, Co-Inventor of ACT!

I gave this book to all of my clients. 5 months later they are still talking about the ideas they are applying."

— John Meetz, President at TAB, Kansas

This book has promoted discussion throughout our organization. -

— Lamar Hunt Jr, Member, Founding Family of the Kansas City Chiefs

Keynote Speaker + Trusted Advisor + Executive Coach

WWW.DARENMARTIN.COM

Contact Dr. Martin via email at

DAREN@DARENMARTIN.COM

For bulk orders or to inquire about our
Act Like An Owner 12 Week Online Course

Please contact - **ELISE@DARENMARTIN.COM**

Tweet us at **@DARENMARTIN** or **@COMPANYOFOWNERS**